"With our attention drawn so consistently toward the global issues that concern the outer environment of life, Hugh Prather's book attends to the inner environment of the unfolding of a person, which is an important accomplishment and counterpoint in the struggle for meaning of our time. It is a useful guide for all those bent on the inner journey, and a helpful companion to the wider orchestration of our interests to create a better world in all respects."

—*Glenn Olds, president, Better World Society*

"From the first moment I opened Hugh Prather's book . . . many years ago . . . his words have been a constant source of joy, inspiration, and comfort *whenever* I read them! . . . In reading of Hugh's search for the truth I was helped to continue my *own* search for the 'inner' voice of truth that is within us all! . . . *Notes to Myself* has radiated out across the whole world, and touched hearts *everywhere*!"

—*Joan Walsh Anglund, artist, poet, and author of* A Friend Is Someone Who Likes You

"*Notes to Myself* is one of those books you never outgrow. You read it again and again every so often and marvel at how much deeper it gets as the years go by."

—*Marianne Williamson, founder, The Centers For Living*

W9-BVL-040

Twentieth Anniversary Edition

NOTES TO MYSELF

My Struggle to Become a Person

Hugh Prather

Bantam Books

New York   Toronto   London   Sydney   Auckland

to
Carl Rogers
(whose *On Becoming A Person*
showed me where to look)

NOTES TO MYSELF
A Bantam Book
published by arrangement with
the author

PUBLISHING HISTORY
Real People Press edition published 1970
Bantam paperback edition / June 1976
Bantam Anniversary rack edition / March 1990
Bantam Anniversary trade edition / May 1990

All rights reserved.
Copyright © 1970 by Real People Press.
Foreword copyright © 1990 by Hugh Prather.
Cover art copyright © 1990 by Claudia Stevens.

Designed by M'N O Production Services, Inc.

No part of this book may be reproduced or transmitted
in any form or by any means, electronic or mechanical,
including photocopying, recording, or by any information
storage and retrieval system, without permission in writing from
the publisher.
For information address: Bantam Books.

If you purchased this book without a cover you should be aware that this
book is stolen property. It was reported as "unsold and destroyed" to
the publisher and neither the author nor the publisher has received any
payment for this "stripped book."

ISBN 978-0-553-27382-3

Published simultaneously in the United States and Canada

Bantam Books are published by Bantam Books, a division of Random House, Inc.
Its trademark, consisting of the words "Bantam Books" and the portrayal of a rooster,
is Registered in U.S. Patent and Trademark Office and in other countries. Marca
Registrada. Bantam Books, New York, New York.

PRINTED IN THE UNITED STATES OF AMERICA

OPM   44   43   42

I started putting *Notes to Myself* together in 1968. Gayle and I had been married just four years. We were living in Berkeley, and it was that period when the flower children moved from Haight-Ashbury to Telegraph Avenue, and lost their way. The ideal that all people should be allowed to "do their own thing," an ideal, really, of complete acceptance, quickly deteriorated into angry, judgmental riots between "heads" and "short hairs." When the war reached our neighborhood on Eighth Avenue, we decided to accept a job on a ranch in Colorado. So in the summer of 1969, in the mountains near Chama, I cleaned out beaver dams and Gayle cleaned cabins, and in my spare time, I finished the manuscript and began the seemingly hopeless process of submitting it to publishers.

Everything I had written in the two years I had been a writer—poems, short stories, humorous articles— had been rejected, and so when I received a letter back from Real People Press within a couple of days of mailing the manuscript, I knew it was a rejection slip. Obviously, they had not had time to read it. I found out later that after finishing the book late the night before, the publisher had gone straight to a mailbox with a letter of acceptance.

John Stevens (now Steve Andreas) turned out to be the most honest publisher with whom I have ever had dealings. His opening sentence began, "You can probably receive a higher royalty from a larger company . . . " Several years later he called me one day and said that he didn't think he was paying me enough (an above-average 10 percent!) and was raising the royalty and making it retroactive for the year. This little press, a husband-and-wife team who had published only three other books, had no salesmen, ran no ads, and didn't even have distribution on the East Coast. Nevertheless, after a few years of the book working its way across country by word of mouth, they found that they had a best-seller. It is now published by Bantam in many foreign languages and has sold several million copies, but I am convinced that Real People Press is the only publisher in the country who would have taken it at that time.

Now, twenty years later, Gayle and I have just written *Notes to Each Other*, and as we have been reviewing the two books, we have been encouraged with at least one obvious fact about progress: In our hearts, we can all sense the way home—even in youth.

Most children perceive the mistakes their parents are making, attitudes and approaches that make life harder rather than easier. "It doesn't have to be this way" is a common childhood feeling that many of us can recall having. Coming into the world already knowing that *it's happier to be happy*, children recognize well and resist with surprising persistence such insane lessons as *it's necessary to be rushed* (instead of simply moving quickly), *it's necessary to be discouraged at night* (instead of simply being tired), *it's necessary to be irritated at mistakes* (instead of simply correcting them), *it's necessary to be discontent with conditions* (instead of taking steps toward a change).

Insights such as these are the little windows onto truth with which we begin life, and that, despite our best efforts, become spotted with the numerous distortions that a young child needing approval cannot help taking on. In many ways life is the process of cleaning the windows until finally we see with understanding what before was sensed only with childlike instinct. Maturity is wanting nothing but what we see with the purity of our heart.

Notes to Myself is the journal of a young man whose personality is yet unformed and whose approach is yet untested. I was plagued with questions of career, sexual expression, feelings of inadequacy, and especially a longing to know oneness with Gayle and all others. My childhood had not prepared me to function well in the world, and I was struggling with loyalty to our marriage, a need for friends, and a deep confusion as to which among the many voices within me was the truest guide.

As were many others of that era, Gayle and I were trying to understand our individual functions in the larger world as well as the smaller world of Berkeley, and not merely to march in step with the old ways of the generation with which we had grown up. Yet we soon discovered that this preoccupation with "actualizing" the self could also lead to egocentricity, and it took an enormous and persistent effort for us to begin applying these insights in a broader, more humane manner.

In a sense, *Notes to Myself* clarified our way, for after it was published a small but steady number of alcoholic and suicidal individuals began turning to us for help. This eventually led to our taking up crisis counseling on a full-time basis. At first, as well as the suicidal, we dealt primarily with battered women and rape victims, but gradually found ourselves working more and more with parents in grief. We started a group for anyone who had had a child die, and unexpectedly began receiving weekly instruction from the people we thought we were there to help. The profound goodness and deep honesty of these parents consolidated and reinforced the simple lessons of our lives.

We put what we had learned from this crisis work in another "Notes" entitled *Notes on How to Live in the World . . . And Still Be Happy*. This in turn led to our work with couples committed to forming long-term relationships and the writing of *A Book for Couples*, for which *Notes to Each Other* is the diary or raw source material.

Notes to Myself was essentially a stack of yellow sheets (which I called my diary) where I went to sort things out, where I put down my pains and problems, and my very deep longing to break through to some truth. In many of the passages I was guessing, but because I was trying hard to be honest with myself, I sometimes guessed right. That is why, aside from some editing and a few additions, I have left the book essentially as it was. In going over each passage, I can remember almost every thought I had when I wrote it— and here's something that is interesting to me—I can *remember* whether I was being dishonest while telling myself that I wasn't. It's especially these little dishonesties that I have corrected.

Now, as well as talking to Gayle and using a diary to sort things out, I sometimes talk to our two boys, Jordan, six, and John, who is ten. Here again is the example that even at a very young age we can all sense the way home. Last week I was putting the six-year-old to bed, and referring to all my burdens I said, "Jordan, *how* can I live a happy life?" Without hesitation he answered, "Do what you say."

Since writing *Notes To Myself*, I guess all I have really been trying to do is just that—*live* the gentle approach it contains. I hope that this little book also echoes the truth of your own path. And please know, I walk with you.

Hugh Prather
May 1989
Santa Cruz, California

NOTES TO MYSELF

    If I had only . . .
forgotten future greatness
and looked at the green things and the buildings
and reached out to those around me
and smelled the air
and ignored the forms and the self-styled obligations
and heard the rain on the roof
and put my arms around my wife
        . . . and it's not too late

She may die before morning. But I have been with her for four years. There's no way I could be cheated if I didn't have her for another day. I didn't deserve her for one minute, God knows.

And I may die before morning.

What I must do is die now. I must accept the justice of death and the injustice of more "life." I have had a good life—longer than many, better than most. Tony died when he was twenty. I have had thirty-two years. I couldn't justify another day. I did not create myself, it is a gift. I am me, *that* is the miracle. I had no right to remain a single hour. Some remain a single minute. And yet I have had thirty-two years.

Few consciously choose when they will die. I choose to accept death now. As of this moment I give up my "right" to live. And I give up my "right" to her life.

But it's morning. Within my hands is
another day. Another day to listen and love
and walk and glory. I am here for another day.

I think of those who aren't.

What does it mean to be here? What does it mean to
have friends? What does it mean to get dressed, to
have a meal, to work? What does it mean to come
home? What is the difference between the living and
the dead?

I sometimes wonder if the "dead" are not more
present, more comfort, more here than most of the
living.

Today I want to do things to be doing them,
not to be doing something else. I don't want
to drive to get there, make love to have
climaxes, or study to "keep abreast."

I don't want to do things to sell myself on
myself. I don't want to do nice things for
people so that I will be "nice." I don't want
to work to make money, I want to work to
work.

Today I don't want to live for,
I want to live.

My prayer is: I will be what I will be,
I will do what I will do.

All I want to do, need to do, is stay in
rhythm with myself. All I want is to do
what I do and not try to do what I don't
do. Just do what I do. Just keep pace
with myself. Just be what I will be.

I will be what I will be—and I am *now*
what I am. Here is where I will devote
my energy. My power is with me, not with
tomorrow. I will work in rhythm with
myself, not with what I "should" be. And
to work in rhythm with myself I must stay
deeply connected to myself. Tomorrow is
shallow, but today is as deep as truth.

God revealed his name to Moses, and it was
I AM WHAT I AM.

I'm convinced that this anxiety running through my life is the tension between what I "should be" and what I am. My anxiety doesn't come from thinking about the future but from wanting to control it. It seems to begin whenever I smuggle into my mind an expectation about how I or others should be. It is the tension between my desire to control the world and the recognition that I can't. "I will be what I will be"—where is the anxiety in that? Anxiety is the recognition that I might not reach the rung on the opinion-ladder I have just set for myself. I fear death most when I am about to exceed what I believe others think of me; then death threatens to cut me off from myself, because "myself" is not yet.

I can't "make my mark" for all time—those concepts are mutually exclusive. "Lasting effect" is a self-contradictory term. Meaning does not exist in the future and neither do I. Nothing I see will have meaning "ultimately." Nothing will even mean tomorrow what it did today. Meaning changes with the context. *My* meaningfulness is here. It's enough that I am of comfort to someone today. It's enough that I make a difference now.

"What do I want to be in life?" Here I assume a *reason* for living that is separate from life. So many now believe their life is headed toward some grand finale. But maybe we are not moving in a direction any more than the world is. The belief that the events of my life are supposed to "add up" causes me to justify my past actions and plan against the future. The reason I don't want to drive, wait in line, run errands for others, is that I think I know what my destiny looks like. This trivial activity is therefore a waste of time because it doesn't contribute to the important work I must do before I die.

The way for me to live is to have no way.
My only habit should be to have none. Because
I did it this way before is not sufficient
reason to do it this way today.

I can have a self or I can have consistent
behavior. I cannot have both.

The key to having "more than enough time"
is to relax. Time is change, therefore I have
more time per clock-hour when I am flexible.
Rigid control means less time because less
change. I can lengthen my life by staying out
of doctrines and ruts.

Confession is often an avoidance of change. If I confess it, I don't have to accept responsibility for changing it: "I confess. It's beyond my control." And it shifts the burden: "You have heard it, now what are *you* going to do about it?"

Deep inner awareness of what I have done and what my motives were can change me. But confession, confrontation, and even spoken forgiveness often get other people entangled in the net of my problem and hinder their freedom as well as complicate mine.

Why do I judge my day by how much I
have "accomplished"?

When I get to where I can enjoy just
lying on the rug picking up lint balls,
I will no longer be too ambitious.

I'm holding this cat in my arms so it can
sleep, and what more is there.

After I had written this book I told several friends. Their reaction was polite and mild. Later I was able to tell them the book was going to be published. Most of them responded with the words "I'm proud of you." Proud of the results but not of the action.

Everyone but I must look *back* on my behavior. They can only see my acts coupled with their results. But I must act *now* without knowing the results. Thus I give my actions their only possible meaning for me. And true meaning always issues from: "I choose to respond to this part of me and not to that part."

I don't live in a laboratory; I have no absolute way of knowing what effects my conduct will have. To live my life for the outcome is to sentence myself to continuous frustration and to hang over my head the threat that death may at any moment make my having lived a waste. My only sure reward is in my actions, not from them. The quality of my reward is in the depth of my response, the centralness of the part of me I act from.

Because the results are unpredictable, no effort of mine is doomed to failure. And even a failure will not take the form I imagine. "It will be interesting to see what happens" is a more realistic attitude toward future consequences than worry. Excitement, dejection, and irritation also assume a knowledge of results that I cannot possess.

If I work toward an end, meantime I am confined to a process.

The rainbow is more beautiful than the pot at the end of it, because the rainbow is now. And the pot never turns out to be quite what I expected.

There is a part of me that wants to write, a part that wants to theorize, a part that wants to sculpt, a part that wants to teach. . . . To force myself into a single role, to decide to be just one thing in life, would kill off large parts of me.

My career will form behind me. All I can do is let this day come to me in peace. All I can do is take the step before me now, and not fear repeating an effort or making a new one.

I say to people, "I always do so-and-so," or
"I never do so-and-so," as if being my *self*
depended on such banal consistencies.

"Next time I will . . ."
"From now on I will . . ."
—What makes me think I am wiser today
than I will be tomorrow?

Boredom or discontent is useful to me when
I acknowledge it and see clearly my
assumption that there's something else
I would rather be doing. In this way
boredom can act as an invitation to freedom
by opening me to new options and thoughts.
For example, if I can't change the activity,
can I look at it more honestly?

The more I consult my deeper feelings
throughout the day, the more I fall back into
that place of quiet knowing to see if what I
am doing is what I want to be doing, then
the less I feel at the end of day that I have
been wasting time. Perhaps the waste was
never in the activities themselves but in my
pulling forth too petty a justification for
doing them.

I have recently noticed that intermittently my mind takes a quick mental survey of my activities up to that point in the day in order to determine my progress. This process is spontaneous, almost unconscious, and seems inherent. If what I have done does not appear to further my advancement, I feel slightly depressed and enervated, and I sense a desire to head in a destructive direction: for example, to go, really *go*, to pot. Any direction seems preferable to no direction at all. But that is not the actual alternative.

Discouragement, if pursued, is the exercise of an option: to turn from creative to noncreative mental activity, to turn from what is present to what is over, to turn from that which builds to that which destroys. By becoming conscious of the option my mood sets before me, I am free to decline it.

As I look back on my life, one of the most constant and powerful things I have experienced is the desire to be more than I am at the moment—an unwillingness to let my mind remain in the pettiness where it idles—a desire to increase the boundaries of my self—a desire to feel more, learn more, express more—a desire to grow, improve, purify, expand. I used to interpret this inner push as meaning that there was some one thing out there that I wanted to do or be or have. And I have spent too much of my life trying to find it. But now I know that this energy within me is seeking more than *the* mate or *the* profession or *the* religion, more even than pleasure or power or meaning. It is seeking more of me; or better, it is, thank God, *releasing* more of me.

The past is over and the future is not yet. My desires must therefore be in and for the present. "I want to lose twenty pounds" means, at most, that the immediate reality of my body and the way I picture myself conflict. Thinking that desires are for the future blocks me from accepting responsibility for my present focus on dissatisfaction, and may cause me to make unnecessary rules about tomorrow.

Often my desires are based on images of what I think I want to be: "I want to work out a theory of reality based on precognition." Is this a desire to do something *today*? If so, what? Regardless of the subject of the desire, what does it push me to do *now*? To drink? To turn away from Gayle? To leave work early? This effect is what the desire is "for."

Perfectionism is slow death. Idols and ideals are based on the past. If everything were to turn out just as I would want it to, just as I would plan, I would never experience anything new. My life would be an endless repetition of stale successes. When I make a mistake I experience something unexpected.

I sometimes react to mistakes as if I have betrayed myself. My fear of them seems to arise from the assumption that I am potentially perfect and that if I can just be very careful I will not fall from heaven. But a mistake is a declaration of the way I am now, a jolt to the expectations I have unconsciously set, a reminder I am not dealing with the facts. When I have *listened* to my mistakes I have grown.

When I see I am doing it wrong, a part of me wants to keep on doing it the same way and even starts looking for reasons to justify the continuation. And no one can tell me better— not even me!

Guilt is a guide that will lead me whenever I choose to follow. It will raise its righteous banner and take me to the wasteland of my incompetence. Guilt is a voice that will speak whenever I choose to listen. It will mournfully address any subject but one: correcting the mistake.

A sure way for me to have a disastrous
experience is to do something because
"it will be good for me."

The key to motivation is to look at how
far I have come rather than how far I have
to go.

Just when I think I have learned the way to live, life changes and I am left the same as I began. The more things change the more I am the same. It appears that my life is a constant irony of maturity and regression, but my sense of progress is based on the illusion that things out there are going to remain the same and that, at last, I have gained a little control. But there will never be means to ends, only means. And I am means. I am what I started with, and when it is all over I will be all that is left of me.

If there is a me that curses and struggles and a me that winks and walks in peace, do I have a choice of selves?

There are occasions when I talk to a man who is riding high on some recent insight or triumph, and for the moment life probably seems to him to have no problems. But I just don't believe that most people are living the smooth, controlled, trouble-free existence that their careful countenances and bland words suggest. Today never hands me the same thing twice and I believe that for almost everyone else life is also a mixture of unsolved problems, ambiguous victories, and vague defeats—with very few moments of clear peace. I never do seem to quite get on top of it. My struggle with today is worthwhile, but it's a struggle nonetheless and one that seems never to end. The payoff must be elsewhere, and I suspect that it's within that laughing heart that can surface so unexpectedly.

Possibly the greatest crime we commit against each other is this daily show of normality. I have countless little conversations with a variety of people and the impression that most of them give is that they don't have problems. Even complainers present themselves as victims. They don't suggest that they may be participating. They are all right; it's circumstances that are wrong.

The comment "Don't mind him, he's got a problem" illustrates this universal attitude toward personal difficulty. The implication is that having a problem is a strange and avoidable weakness. When I come in repeated contact with this daily facade of normality I begin to assume that I too deserve such a life, and I get annoyed with the present and look upon my difficulties as unjust. And because I assume there is something unnatural about my having a problem, I too attempt to present a problem-free appearance.

I live from one tentative conclusion to the next, thinking each one is final. The only thing I know for sure is that I'm confused.

What an absurd amount of energy I have been wasting all my life trying to figure out how things "really are," when all the time they weren't.

Do I really think there is anything more profoundly true about my interpretation of the situation, now that I'm wide awake in bed, than there was when I was in the middle of it this afternoon?

There are no absolutes for something so relative as a human life. There are no rules for something so gentle as a heart.

For me, thinking seems to act at times as a defense mechanism, a way of avoiding some insight, a way of *not* looking at the situation. This is especially true during social encounters, when I tend to lead with my head.

My trouble is I analyze life instead of live it.

A theory is a theory, not a reality. All that a theory can do is remind me of certain thoughts that were part of my reality *then*. A statement or a "fact" is an emphasis—one way of looking at something. At worst it's a kind of myopia. A name is also just one way of seeing. I can't make a statement about a reality without omitting many other aspects that are also true. Even if it were possible to say everything, still I wouldn't have the reality; I would only have the words. In fact, what I see changes even as I describe it.

When I outgrow my names and facts and theories, or when reality leaves them behind, something in me begins to die if I don't continue on toward a broader way of seeing, one in which I look without categorizing, one in which I look, not even for stillness, but from stillness.

I keep thinking I have to do something to shore up reality. Bill and Leah are over here—just let the conversation take place. Don't push. Don't hang on. Lean back and let reality unfold.

I constrict my vision and disregard my options when I pursue. I cannot receive from the unknown when I grasp. Nothing exists for me until I see it. There is little I can do about my feelings, but honesty removes the edge of pain from my wants. And awareness shows me that, miraculously, the universe continues to function without my worry.

Eloquence is sometimes lyrical, sometimes powerful, but unless it includes love, unless the words caress the heart as well as the ear, it is a beauty that inspires but does not heal.

Dishonest people believe in words rather than love.

Anyone who inhabits himself cannot believe in objective thinking.

"I am at peace with myself" leads to the trapdoor at the bottom of the soul, below which is a recognition even more disconcerting than equality: the wordless experience that I am you and you are me.

Now that I know I'm no wiser than anyone else, does this wisdom make me wiser?

The number of things just outside the perimeter of my financial reach remains constant no matter how much my financial condition improves. With each increase in my income a new perimeter forms and I experience the same relative sense of lack. I believe that I know the specific amount needed that would allow me to have or do these few things I can't quite afford, and if my income would increase by that much I would then be happy. Yet when the increase comes, I find that I am still discontent because from my new financial position I can now see a whole new set of things I don't have. The problem will be solved when I accept that happiness is a present attitude, not a future condition.

I don't need a "reason" to be happy. I don't have to consult the future to know how happy I am now.

The thought, "You're lucky, it could have been worse," is the kind of gratitude I can do without. It also could have been better, or, actually, it couldn't have been any other way than the way it was.

At first I thought that to "be myself" meant simply to act the way I feel. I would ask myself a question such as, "What do I want to say to this person?" and very often the answer was surprisingly negative. It seemed that my negative feelings were always the ones I noticed first, possibly because of their social unusualness, possibly because I feared having to act them out. However, as I continued practicing I saw that below these were more positive feelings—if I was still long enough to look deeply. The more I attempted to "be me" the more "me's" I found there were. Now I understand that to be myself means consciously choosing which level of my feelings I am going to respond to and recognizing that, whatever I am feeling, I am always free to think carefully rather than carelessly about myself and those around me. When I am careful about the thoughts I brood on, because thought precedes feeling, circumstances can no longer dictate my mood. But when I think carelessly, my self is "lost in thought."

When I made my first efforts to be true to myself, I felt trapped in a self I didn't like. I thought I was stuck with the emotions I had, that I couldn't change them, and shouldn't try to even if I could. I saw many selfish, cowardly, even cruel feelings that I didn't want, and yet believed that I had to express them if I were going to be myself. I was failing to see that expressing a feeling is how I am to others, not how I am to myself. Not wanting to express negative feelings is also a feeling, a part of me, and if it is the greater part, I will be truer to myself by not expressing them.

An emotion can be changed, but only to a different emotion. I am always feeling something. Many times I have been mired in some tone of life that stretched endlessly on, and any emotion seemed preferable to the dominating one. I discovered that by manipulating circumstances (quitting a job, switching partners, turning against an organization) I could generate anger, infatuation, sadness, excitement, or some other dramatic change in my feelings. Yet I was still making my mind an effect of the world and thereby remaining a victim.

How can I begin unless I see where I'm starting from? I must take up my life as my life is now. Now I am broke, supported by Gayle, a dropout from pigeon psychology, overweight, disowned by both our families because writing is not a "real job," living in a noisy quadraplex in the middle of a Berkeley war zone. Today, this is my life. Will I keep waiting, or will I start with what I have?

Don't fight a fact, deal with it.
Don't discard your self, be more of it.

The bully in me always bullies in the name of principle or in the name of rules. The bully in me acts quite reasonably and regrets that others must suffer as a consequence. This part of me is a coward—it hides behind "what is right" so I won't have to admit my desire to hurt.

I have to become conscious of my desire to hurt *before* I can become conscious of my desire not to hurt. Most mistakes are corrected through increased awareness, which usually does not come without some discomfort.

Most people believe that their greatest weakness is their greatest strength. They attack in others what they themselves do in a different form, and this pattern continues until they become fully conscious of it. To deliberately focus on my insensitivity, judgmentalness, dishonesty, and anger does not make me a more negative person, because the negativity was already there.

Unless I feel within me the potential to commit any act committed by others, I can be controlled by these same urges. Once I recognize that I am feeling them, yet consciously choose not to carry them out, I free myself from this possibility —provided I can also recognize that this is no sacrifice.

At times I want to hurt or intimidate Moosewood. I especially feel this way when she cowers. If I don't try to mentally sidestep these feelings, and if I open my heart to everything else I feel about her, I play with her in a rough way she enjoys.

There is a palpable resistance that must be endured to allow kindness into the eyes, but the result is like the wave of a magic wand. A second before she was an object to be kicked; now she is my dog, with feelings of her own that I want to protect.

If, on the other hand, I avoid my urge to hurt, or try to act nice in spite of it, the urge grows. To ignore my feelings is to condemn myself for having them, and it's as if the rejected part of me reacts by getting nasty.

I don't have to fear any feeling I have.
Even a murderous feeling doesn't make me
a murderer. However, to deny my darker
emotions can have serious consequences.
When I disown a feeling I do not destroy it, I
only forfeit my capacity to act it out as I
wish. Even to think guiltily or irritatedly
about a feeling merely strengthens its hold on
my mind. Yet regardless of the state I am in,
I am always free to draw upon my reserves of
stillness and peace, and whenever I do, the
inner shift is subtle but profound: I become
peacefully depressed, peacefully fearful,
peacefully angry. And whereas the effect of
my mood before was to pull others down with
me, now I leave the world uncontaminated.

If love is at the core of us, we can add
love to any misery we feel.

Tonight a little boy fell into my lap and looked up at me for affection. I felt tight and awkward. I was battling myself so hard over how I "should" feel that I didn't pause long enough to see how I did feel. Maybe the fear that more was expected of me than I had to give was groundless and love would have been there if I had only allowed myself to look.

It's not that we fear the place of darkness but that we don't think we are worth the effort to find the place of light.

When Gayle gets sick I feel judgmental, then angry, then emotionally flat. I feel judgmental: she's making a demand I can't fulfill (I can't quickly fix things up); she's using up my precious time; she's making a messy situation. Then I get angry because I believe that I shouldn't be judgmental merely because someone is sick. Finally, I resign myself and my emotions shut down altogether. If in the middle of this I freeze the contents of my mind, and look at them carefully, I see that these loveless reactions are on the surface and that on another level I have *not* gotten caught up in this same old pattern. It is hard for me to stay in contact with this quieter, gentler self. And I lose sight of it immediately if, before seeing it clearly, I act more sympathetically than I feel.

Self-reproach is a very interesting state—I have the illusion of doing something. However, it's not the process of self-reform it first seems. I have stopped at partial rather than complete acceptance of a fault.

Forgiveness is the willingness to begin. Guilt is the love of staying stuck.

Unless I accept my faults, I will unquestionably doubt my virtues.

Both my body and my emotions were given to me, and it's as futile for me to condemn myself for feeling scared, insecure, or revengeful as it is for me to get mad at myself for the size of my feet. I am not responsible for my feelings, but for what I do with them.

It's as useless for me to be disgruntled over how I was just using my mind as it is for me to criticize myself for thoughts I had ten years ago. Okay, that is what I just thought—now this is what I'm thinking.

"You shouldn't feel that way." My emotions never arise for the limited reasons I think. I don't know what my body "ought" to be feeling because I'm not in a position to see every past experience and present influence from which they arise. My body has reasons of its own to be feeling the way it does, and all things considered (which I cannot do) it couldn't be feeling any other way.

And if I lack the grounds to feel guilty over my own emotions, how can I criticize yours?

"Don't condemn yourself for your feelings."
(Not even for the condemnatory ones?)
"Don't feel bad."
(But I *do*.)
I feel what I feel what I feel.

I have two sets of emotions, one based on the
past, which keeps the world the same, the
other reached only from the present, which is
immune to my habitual interpretations.
Although thought precedes emotion, thoughts
are frequently unconscious, and a given
emotion is often the first clue I have as to
how I have been using my mind. My past-
based thoughts have a natural, random flow,
as do the feelings that follow. The mistake
is to fixate on only one thought or
interpretation, because this instantly makes
me a victim emotionally of what other people
do and say. When I defend my emotions, I am
actually defending the lesser part of my mind.

I was just asked to go somewhere. I said, "I can't. I have to stay home. Gayle's sick." Clearly, I was not accepting responsibility for my actions. Next time I want to be more honest and state that I do what I do because *I* want to do it.

I notice that I sometimes think, "I ought to do so-and-so," in order to hide from my desire to do it. If I "have" to do it, I don't have to admit that I want to, or look at my motive for why I want to.

The injunction to be unselfish refers only to one sense of self. I certainly know what it's like to be preoccupied and uncaring, yet I am also conscious of a deep desire to treat others' feelings as my own. Each of us is selfish in the sense that we are always doing what some part of us wants. Generosity feels at least as rewarding as greed. Selfishness is neither good nor bad—it depends on the *way* we are selfish as to whether it nourishes or injures.

One kind of lie that I tell pops out in conversation and takes me by surprise. It alerts me to the areas where I feel inadequate and could be more accepting of myself. Sometimes I like to correct these lies on the spot, and when I do, contrary to what might be expected, most people do not think less of me. Another kind of lie begins when I believe I can foresee the consequences of something I have done. I start having fantasies about how I am going to explain things, and if these go unobserved, they tend to convince a part of my mind that things happened more advantageously than they did, and I end up telling a lie—half believing it to be true. If I become aware of these fantasies, I can do something that interrupts the pattern: I can get very clear about what did happen and what I would say if I wanted to be truthful. Just doing that much often takes a persistent effort. Afterward, however, I usually want to tell the truth, and if not, I can now see what response would feel least like self-betrayal.

To lie is to consciously communicate a false impression, and this can be done with words that are literally correct. What I want are words that reflect my heart, not my cleverness.

The fantasies that I have in reaction to something that just happened often express how I would like to feel rather than how I do feel. Here's this man I'm afraid of and I fantasize the part of the very tough person—when actually I feel weak in relation to him. Do I want to actualize myself? Okay, the actuality is I'm afraid of him.

When I examine my fantasies for the values they express, I'm surprised at the pettiness. The unstill part of the mind travels from one trivial issue to another, avoiding the present and avoiding love. I don't think the answer is to try to reform it, rather it's to stop taking it so seriously. It's just a soap opera playing in another room, the voices rising, falling, now filled with deceit, now horror, now outrage, now reason. Its effect on me is minimal as long as I don't try to make out the words.

When I am afraid, whether physically, socially, or financially, I do not have to choose between following the dictates of the fear or reacting against them. Fear is neither an intelligence I wish to lead me nor a sin I wish to flee. It is a great churning of thought caused by the object of thought, and only stillness can see past it. However, it is not the fearful thoughts themselves that must be stilled, but thoughts containing stillness that must be brought into focus.

The mind lives in what it sees. The imagery of picturing what size container would be needed to hold the fear, or of describing where in the body the fear is located, are effective because they are ways of putting agitation into the context of stillness, of putting the lesser into the greater.

Fear is static that prevents me from hearing my intuition.

Anxiety, fear, panic, is running away mentally, not physically. There is something over there in the corner of my mind, some thought, some image, that I don't want to look at. Fear is based on the belief that I am safer not seeing, like a child closing its eyes as the ball comes toward it. Awareness is the first step to freeing the mind. I must not only hear the fear out but question it closely as to the answer it is suggesting. Just as with a nightmare, most fears will fall by the weight of their own nonsense—once they are bluntly seen.

If there were no love-based feelings and our only choices were among the feelings that separate—jealousy, discouragement, fear, anger, discontent, lethargy, greed, etc.—there would be no question that each was more appropriate in one set of circumstances than another. It's better to drive a car with fear than with lethargy. It's better to defend a child against a dog with anger than with discouragement. And it probably causes others less pain to dress and groom oneself with a little anxiety than with indifference. However, any feeling that makes me betray my own heart can have only temporary value. Fear, for example, urges me to act before I know what my deeper feelings are: Fear of what I am eating causes me to bolt down my food. Fear of displeasing others causes me to speak too quickly. I feel less a person when I have acted in these unconscious ways. I want to be aware of what others expect but not despotized by it. If I defiantly choose the opposite, I am still being controlled. Whether I am driving, caring for a child, eating, dressing, or conversing, I want to act out of respect for myself and the feelings of others.

The way to be most helpful to others is for me to do the thing that right now would be most helpful to me.

The ancient wisdom, "To give is to receive," is usually interpreted as giving first to others. Yet love sends warmth in all directions, and if giving is receiving, receiving must also be giving. The real question is, What can be truly given?

I am not interested so much in what I do with my hands or words as what I do with my heart. I want to live from the inside out, not from the outside in.

Most words evolved as a description of the separated realities of the external world, hence their inadequacy to describe the one gentle reality within us all.

Wanting to do something is a desire, not a sentence. When I "decide" what I want, I translate my desire into a sentence and then follow the sentence; I take the desire out of my heart and put it into my ego. Asking myself, "What should I do?" brings to mind my habitual answers to that question, it brings in what the voices from my past would want me to do, and it ignores the fact that there are probably no adequate words to describe where my heart is leading me this instant.

The configuration of most situations implies, through tradition, a corresponding emotion: We look at all we have to do and feel overwhelmed. Our spouse flirts and we feel jealous. Someone takes the parking place we are backing into and we feel enraged. We are not invited and we feel slighted. Added to traditional interpretations are countless other factors dictating how we should feel: the habitual responses we picked up from our parents, the mood we are in at the time, the attitudes of the other people involved, the religious or ethical tradition we learned as a child. Thus, in reality, we can and do respond quite differently to the same provocation each time it occurs.

The "shoulds" in how I "should" feel conflict to the point of anxiety, which is how I feel much of the time. Only the stillness of my heart is consistent, and it does not dictate how to behave but merely how to see.

If I want to clarify what it is I wish to do about this situation, it would be helpful to be certain I know the difference between how I see this man and how everyone is telling me he is. *I* do not see Rudy as malicious. How do I see him? Here I run into the problem of how I really see him versus trying to remain consistent with how I told everyone I saw him. I can be faithful to my image or faithful to myself.

I can get more directly at what I am feeling
most deeply if I think "I" instead of "you"
and stop talking to myself in the third person.
The third person postulates an audience and so
tends to elevate how I appear over how I am.

Analysis is condemnation. I ask myself, "Why do you want to do *that*?" This question is ill willed. I am seeking a motive that I have prejudged unworthy of me. Second-guessing my motives undermines faith in my own mind and leads to a decision to thwart the desire I had. A healthier approach would be to accept the desire and simply seek to learn its direction, seek to clarify it rather than judge it.

Most decisions, possibly all, have already been made on a deeper level than the sentence level of the mind, and my going through a reasoning process to arrive at them seems at least redundant. The question, "What do I want to do?" may often be a fearful reaction to the unconscious decision I have already made. It's quite different from "What do I *really* want to do?" or "What am I really feeling?" These questions acknowledge that at any given moment I am experiencing a variety of thoughts and emotions and that what I want is the state which is most central to me. If I can experience that then what to do will be obvious and probably will follow naturally.

If I feel angry I don't have to ask what I want to do, because on the level of the anger the decision is already in place to make someone feel guilty. And on the level of my core, if I feel love, the decision is already made to act *without* harming. The question, therefore, is not what to do, but where within me am I looking.

Sometimes the only way for me to discover what I want to do is to go ahead and do something. Then when I start to act, my feelings begin to clarify. This much, however, is certain: When I act from fear or when I act from condemnation, the results contain a disturbance.

Being myself includes taking risks with myself, taking risks on new behavior, trying new ways of thinking and being, so I can come to know how it feels to walk hand-in-hand with my self.

If the desire to write is not accompanied
by actual writing then the desire is not
to write.

Standing before the refrigerator:
If I have to ask myself if I'm hungry,
I'm not.

Someone asks: Would you like to do so-and-so? A picture forms in my mind and as I look at it, it is appealing or unappealing and I say yes I would or no I wouldn't. Yet this picture is not precognitive. It is a composite of past experiences that will be more or less *unlike* the coming event.

There is no way to *know* which future course is best because there is no way to foresee all those my decision will affect and how it will affect them, and to attempt to force my mind to reach certainty only assures that it will not. Yet it's always possible to know what I *believe* would be best, because belief is found in the present. My task, therefore, is not to "see my way through," but merely to discover my deepest preference.

I experience something in my life that is so tangible that I'm puzzled there is no word for it. Others I have talked to also experience it, some more strongly than I. It is the feeling of "now is the time to do it." Often when I am asked why I haven't done something, the answer is I haven't gotten this go-ahead. The astronauts receive a signal that comes close to describing it: "All systems are GO." —But they at least can tell you where it's coming from.

My intuitive sense of the natural, right thing to do under the circumstances—when I am quiet enough to hear it—seems somehow to take future circumstances into consideration. I feel "Do this," and it is only afterwards that I see the sense of it. The "sense," however, is not in everything working out the way I would like, but in always receiving an efficient and needed lesson in increased awareness.

To listen to my intuition is to identify with my entire awareness, to *be* my entire experience, and not just my conscious perception. My total awareness synthesizes into a calm sense of direction that is above reason.

It is only when my attention becomes fixated that I act like an unknowing part rather than a knowing whole. When I favor my conscious perception over my total awareness, I can no longer hear the guiding rhythm of one whole reality.

Calmness accompanies the whole. Fear accompanies the part. Intuition looks beyond the latest object of my concern to see the stillness of all outcomes.

It is sometimes said that each of us is ultimately alone. That idea is compelling not because of birth and death but because so often our moments alone seem more true, more real. The word "God" only begins to have meaning for me when I am alone. Or if not alone, so at one with another that there is no sense of a competing reality. God has no meaning for me in a discussion. I don't think religion is an attainable subject for the intellect. I can only believe when I'm not talking about it.

I need solitude like I need food and rest, and like eating and resting, solitude is most healing when it fits the rhythm of my needs. A rigidly scheduled aloneness does not nourish me.

Solitude is perhaps a misnomer. To me, being alone means togetherness—the re-coming-together of myself and nature, of myself and being; the reuniting of my self with all other selves. Solitude especially means putting the parts of my mind back together, unifying the pieces of my self scattered by anger and fear, until I can once again see that the little things are little and the big things are big.

When I was "religious," at times I got very confusing results when I tried to rely continuously on my intuition to guide me. This suggests to me now that I should use my intuition when it feels appropriate, use meditation when it feels appropriate, use reasoning when it seems natural, and so forth. It is absurdly contradictory to believe I must always rely on my intuition because I have *reasoned out* that this is best.

The tools of the mind can be wrongly used, but the mind possesses no wrong tools.

For the last week I have been playing a game. I have been trying to predict what I would be doing in five minutes or in two minutes. I have found that no matter how hard I try I am more often wrong than right, and when I'm right it's obvious that this outcome has been reached so precariously that the results seem accidental. I have also been struck with the radical difference between my fantasy about the future and the actual experience. My prediction is at most a vague picturing of a *category* of activity, whereas the experience itself is made up of mood, thoughts, bodily sensations, detailed perceptions, etc., none of which is exactly like what I have experienced before. I have discovered that when I am conscious of the radical unpredictability of the future—even the immediate future—I find it impossible to be discontent. Discontent seems to be a false concept of time. It leans on my expectation that what is to come will be "the same old thing." I cannot expect imminent change and remain judgmental of the present.

I am noticing that when I am bored I think I am tired of my surroundings but I am really tired of my thoughts. It is trite, repetitious, unobserved thinking that is producing the discontent. Adopting a quiet awareness, a kind of listening attitude, usually freshens my mind and brings the situation I am in to life.

Dishonesty splits the mind. If my attention is wandering, there is somewhere it wants to go, so obviously it does not want to be where I am holding it in the name of some self-imposed duty.

A plan eliminates discontent by promising change. But, ironically, a plan is only my decision to *imagine* a different future, and if followed too rigidly it blocks my sensitivity to the people around me.

Sometimes my discontent works like this: I don't like what I am doing and can't think of an acceptable alternative. My mind fantasizes one unsatisfactory plan after another and my discontent deepens. When this happens I find it helpful to suspend my efforts to "decide." Believing that my intellect alone must choose makes my body into an object and splits me. If I pause and become very aware of the flow of feelings inside me, I presently sense an impulse from more deeply within quietly directing me what to do, or I notice that I have already acted, and that "deciding" was not a part of it. Sometimes the "what to do" is to put my entire self ("pour myself") into what I am already doing, in other words, to bring all of me into the present.

It is not always necessary to think words. Words often keep me from acting in a fully conscious way. Fear, indecision, and condemnation feed on words. Without words they usually die. When I am trying to figure out how I should relate to someone, especially a stranger, if I will stop thinking words, and listen to the situation, and just be open, I find that I act in a more appropriate, more spontaneous, often original, sometimes even courageous way. Words are at times good for calling the mind back, but they are distracting when I need to respond to the present.

It is 9:58 and it is now. Tomorrow at 3:00 it will be now. On my deathbed it will still be now. Since it will always be now, learning to respond to now is the only thing there is to learn.

When I'm critical of another person, when I see his behavior as a "fault," my attitude includes these feelings: I think of him as one thing (instead of having many parts). I dislike him. I "just can't understand" his action. I think he "knows better." And I think he has a choice. If I feel this way I am in reality seeing my own self-condemnation. "Fault" means failure to meet a standard. Whose? Mine. Another person's behavior is "bad" or "understandable" according to my experience with *myself*. My feeling of censure means that if *I* had acted that way I would think of myself as selfish, opinionated, immature, etc. A part of me wants to act that way or thinks of myself as acting that way and condemns this. If I could see clearly why I also behave like that, or want to, and was no longer attacking myself for it, I wouldn't be critical of this person now. I'm getting upset because there is something in me I don't understand and haven't yet accepted.

Forgiveness lifts my curse on myself so that I no longer see it projected on another.

Simply because they had not paid all their rent, Lorson tried to have Mac and Laurie charged with a felony. I feel disgust for him. I consider him a devious weakling. He seems like something that should be stepped on.

But if he had shot them what would I have felt? Probably not anger; but a gangster in my place might have felt anger. If Lorson had cannibalized them I would not have felt anger at all but shock, amazement, and possibly even a kind of pity for him.

The principle seems to be: It's a fault if I am also capable of it, a disease if I am not.

If I feel disapproval of someone, if I find myself ignoring or turning away from someone in a group, I am probably avoiding in myself what this person represents that I believe is true about me.

If something you do *rankles* me, I can know that, however differently you choose to express it, your fault is my fault too.

The criticism that hurts the most is the one that echoes my own self-condemnation.

I have two principal ways of discovering the areas where I fail to see myself. The first is acknowledging the qualities in others that irritate me. The second is acknowledging the comments that have made me defensive. To discover what irritates me, I merely review my latest encounters, but I have more difficulty recognizing when I am defensive. I can sometimes identify it by the following syndrome: I answer quickly. I feel an urge to say more than I need to. I explain, try to persuade, and feel impatient when interrupted. I feel frustrated even if I appear to succeed, as if the damage has already been done. I am incapable of taking the other people's comments any way but seriously; their words never seem light or funny (yet when my reaction becomes apparent, *they* often take the situation lightly).

If it's afterwards that my defensiveness surfaces (usually because I have been chewing on what was said) my mental state has these characteristics: I think hurriedly. I think in circles, replaying the scene and endlessly revising my part. I look for ways to justify attacking back—never fully admitting my true motive. And I feel a strong resistance to stopping and implementing a procedure (any procedure) that would change my mental tone.

Now that I know that when I criticize another I am seeing my own fault, I like to be very honest and very *specific* in my criticism. After I get it straight how I think this fault works in someone else, I can then look at my own behavior with a surprising new clarity. (This way of criticizing works best when I do it silently.)

When I feel defensive, if I will remain aware of my defensiveness and yet be careful not to push the other person to behave in a way that would justify my desire to attack, I can *continue* being responsible for my own defensiveness.

No one is wrong. At most someone is uninformed. If I think an individual is wrong, either I am unaware of something, or the person is. So unless I want to play a superiority game I had best find out what he or she is looking at.

"You're wrong" means that I don't understand you, I'm not seeing what you're seeing—and I'm not seeing all of you there is to see. But there is nothing *wrong* with you. You are where you need to be, doing what you need to be doing, and although I may take steps to protect myself or others, I do not know *all* and therefore am literally inadequate to judge.

I always seem to be feeling either superior or inferior, one up or one down, better off or worse off than everyone else. The superior moments are elating, but the rare and blessed moments are when I feel equal.

There is no such thing as "best" in a world of individuals.

Why this need to divide up, classify, and neatly
package every new acquaintance? For me to try
to classify something so complex as an
individual human merely demonstrates my own
shallowness. A judgment of another person is an
abstraction that adds qualities which are not
there and leaves out what is unique. When I
classify individuals I turn them into objects.
The only way for me to contact other people is
to experience them, not think about them.

This: It's such a chore to talk to Bill. Why is he such a drag?

Versus this: I make such a chore for myself when I talk to Bill. How do I make it so hard?

The way to resolve this need to share my marital troubles with a friend and still remain loyal to Gayle is to express them as mine and not as caused by her. It is equally important to choose carefully the friend to whom I speak, because the mere act of talking *about* our relationship distances me from it, especially if I know in my heart that the listener will take my side.

When Bruce said he had trouble getting
along with his mother, I liked him better.
I like a man with faults, especially when
he knows it. To err is human—I'm
uncomfortable around gods.

I have the choice of being right
or being human.

If I meet someone I have been criticizing I
am usually nicer than I feel.
Being careless toward
another leads to being careless
toward myself.

It is impossible to make a general statement that covers every exception. And yet discussions and arguments so often consist of each person pointing out the obvious exceptions to the other person's statements.

I can't legitimately disagree with what you say about yourself, only with what you say about what is not yourself. The most I can answer to what you say about yourself is that I'm different.

The statements that communicate most clearly are about me, you, now, here; and all final authorities are present.

A generalization is an assertion that what is true for me is also true for not-me. I notice that I often talk in generalities to produce the illusion that my "truth" is shared. In this way I pick up a little support (sameness) for my individuality and don't feel so alone.

Sometimes when I generalize I am saying, "Let's pretend I'm God," and of course the other person argues that point endlessly. Yet I notice that when people simply trust themselves enough to state their thoughts as *their thoughts*, I not only pay more attention to what they are saying, but it helps me look deeper into myself.

If you will tell me the way *you* see it rather than the way it "is," this helps me discover more fully the way I see it.

Whenever I find myself arguing for something with great passion, I can be certain I'm not convinced.

I find it almost impossible to make a strong declarative statement in conversation without feeling little nagging doubts and reservations.

"I agree" and "I disagree" are impossible states of mind. No two people can think exactly alike or antithetically. Sometimes I say "I agree" because I want to avoid an encounter; sometimes I just want to get the other person to shut up. I usually say "I disagree" when I want to exhibit myself.

There is an important difference between telling myself how I experience another person and adding arguments to support the correctness of my view. My feelings about another do not require a case—I don't notice them deductively.

When someone disagrees with me, I do not have to immediately start revising what I just said.

People don't want me to always agree with them. They can sense this is phony. They can sense I am trying to control them: I am agreeing with them to make them like me. They feel: "I don't want to exist to like you. I DON'T exist to like you."

I don't exist to like, but I do exist to love. Contrary to liking, love demands nothing in return.

When I am feeling small, negative feedback seems better than none. I would rather have a person hate me than overlook me. As long as I am hated I make a difference.

Hunting, throwing stones at wildlife, buying exotic pets, picking flowers, criticizing prominent people, may at times be an attempt to make contact with, even identify with, that which seems free and beautiful and so frightfully unlike us.

When people criticize me I am not any less
because of that. It is not a criticism of
me but critical thinking from them. They
are expressing their thoughts and feelings,
not my being.

Before, I thought I was actually fighting
for my own self-worth; that is why I so
desperately wanted people to like me. I
thought their liking me was a comment on
me, but it was a comment on them.

The question I could ask myself after receiving criticism is, "Does this statement give me any insight into myself?" not "Is it true?" If I say, "That's true," those words really mean, "I think about myself in the same way." No one is in a position to know whether or not it *is* true.

A criticism is at best a description of the immediate past. It does not describe the future course of a life. So is it true to how I have been or true to what I will be? And more importantly, to which end will I use it?

"What an ass I made of myself."—No, *I* didn't make the impression. It was her impression of me. I don't come across as any one thing. I don't predetermine a set reaction. There are any number of ways people can react to what I do. How they choose to react is their responsibility. (This is a little harder to see if I "make a big hit.")

I don't *have* to react to criticism with hurt feelings. It's my interpretation of *the meaning for me* that produces the pain. Bob says, "Sometimes you act like a three-year-old," or Esther says, "You sound like a preacher." What meaning do these comments have for me? I am the one who must choose to interpret them as derogatory; they are not inherently so. I am the one who must make the connection and call it bad. I believe that if I were more fully conscious and acceptant of the way I am, and if I were more familiar with how I am "at heart," I would not feel so criticized or complimented by people's words but would be confident to judge their accuracy for myself.

Insecurity can mean lack of self-knowledge: I am not secure with myself—I can't rely on myself—I don't know how I operate. I am insecure to the degree I keep parts of myself hidden from myself.

Or insecurity can mean I know how I operate but don't think it's good enough. When I find myself mentally rehearsing how I should act, how I should *present* myself, this shows that I lack respect for the way I am—I can't be trusted to be perfect and so I have to make rules. Otherwise, I just might slip and be a human being.

The need to "build myself up" is probably what makes me, Paul, etc., talk excessively. The fear that I'm not much prompts me because there have been times in the past when the right words have wowed people—"If I can just say the right words these people will like me."

Bragging is a half-hidden, matter-of-fact rehearsal of past accomplishments, which I usually slip into the conversation under false pretenses—as opposed to the excited sharing of some recent recognition or achievement with a friend. But even with friends, I notice that it's kinder to be very intuitive as to whether the news will be happily received, *before* I say it.

Last night I started using swear words with Bill when I thought I was sounding nicer than I felt. Evidently I want to swear in order to become more real—or is it to sound more real?

When I swear, I am being something rather than saying something.

Profanity fixes the other person's attention on my words rather than my thoughts.

It could be that if I were not afraid to just be myself, I would be naturally funny. It could be that a humorous response does flick through my mind, but fear of what people might think if I just blurted out my thoughts kills it.

True humor is fun—it does not put down, kid, or mock. It makes people feel wonderful, not separate, different, and cut off. True humor has beneath it the understanding that we are all in this together.

My saying "and" and "uh" results from my need to answer immediately, to speak without any break, as if taking time to know what I want to say were embarrassing.

Interpreting the pause is *their* problem.

If I feel compelled to answer every question, *I* am the one compelling me.

Maybe I'd better not talk anymore, he may be tired of listening to me. But I am talking because *I* want to, because it's doing something for *me*, not because it's doing something for him. So the question is do *I* want to talk some more. If I want to stop talking out of kindness, that decision is not forced on me but is also my responsibility.

I want to say something to this person but the fear comes: "I'd better not" (she may misunderstand, she may be in a hurry, ad infinitum). These fears are not based on the present situation, they are based on the past, and I don't have to be governed by what *once* went wrong. The two of us are standing here in the present. What is the situation *now*?

There is something about compliments that scares me. Part of the reason may be that I'm afraid of getting something that can be subsequently taken away. I put myself in the hands of other people if I let my emotions lean on their statements.

Another reason: I am being put on the spot and now must watch what I do to keep them thinking this way about me.

Another: There is a part of me that knows I am not as good as their compliments imply.

Another: I have often been insincere when saying similar things.

Flattery can stir me up as much as criticism —if I take it to heart.

Both Bill and Bob have accused me of wanting to make them my father when I have complimented them excessively. What motivates me to blow up another person bigger than life? Possibly it's because I see this good in them and want it to be all-in-all. I want to lose myself in it. I don't know that it's bad, just unnecessary. It's looking to the limited for the unlimited. It seems very similar to becoming infatuated with a beautiful woman.

The way to handle praise is honestly. Laurel said, "You are one of the kindest people I have ever known." I could have said, "I believe I am kind but not as kind as you see me. We have known each other only a short time and I have been putting my best foot forward. After you know me better I believe you will agree I can be as thoughtless as the next guy."

My friendship with Laurel seems to typify a dynamic that many of my newly forming friendships go through. At first we saw only each other's virtues. Now we are seeing only each other's faults. If we make it through this latter stage, maybe we will see each other and truly be friends.

Interests change. Friendship based on mutual interests is doomed. Real friendship is an unshakable faith in what was once truly seen, no matter how recently or long ago.

Sometimes my contacts with people, even people I'm close to, are frustrating. Afterwards I feel dissatisfied, or sad, or even slightly irritated as if I have been wasting time. Surely these feelings must arise from a thwarting of my expectations. I go wanting something from the person and do not get it. Things I might want: approval, help, fun, entertainment (escape from boredom), recognition, love, sex, justification.

If I went wanting to be a friend rather than to have one, my want could not be frustrated.

If I need your approval I can't see you.

I need approval, but now that I'm no longer
a child I don't have to get it from any one
individual.

Dislike is a function of need. I want
something from you that you don't provide and
so I dislike that condition and call you bad.
The squirrel who lives behind our cabin
becomes furious whenever I empty the
garbage. I don't need his approval and his
anger amuses me. But if he were my pet and I
needed his cooperation then this same anger
would irritate me. I don't dislike a stone
unless it's in my path, or a cloud unless it
rains on me. If I feel in need of something
from you then I hear your words only as yes,
no, maybe, or irritatingly off the subject. I
cannot appreciate you as you are and cannot
begin to see the world as you see it.

Most conversations seem to be carried out on two levels, the verbal and the emotional. The verbal level contains those things that are socially acceptable to say, but it is used as a means of satisfying emotional needs. Yesterday a friend related something that someone had done to her. I told her why I thought the person had acted the way he had and she became very upset and started arguing with me. Now, the reason is clear. I had been listening to her words and had paid no attention to her feelings. Her words had described how terribly this other person had treated her, but her emotions had been saying, "Please understand how I felt. Please accept my feeling the way I did." The last thing she wanted to hear from me was an explanation of the other person's behavior.

I talk because I feel, and I talk to you because I want you to know how I feel.

My statements are requests.

My questions are statements.

My trivia is an invitation to be friends.

My gossip is a plea: Please see me as incapable of that. Please respect me.

My arguments insist: I want you to show respect for me by agreeing with me. This is the way *I* say it is.

And my criticism informs you: You hurt my feelings a minute ago.

If I ignore the emotional plea and respond only to the words, I will not be communicating with you, there will not be a flow of understanding between us, I will not be feeling you and so I will be frustrated and you will be also. The heart of any conversation is the demand being made on my capacity for understanding. If I feel frustrated, that is a good sign I am avoiding the emotions you are trying to communicate—I have not paused long enough to ask, "What do you *really* want from me?"

I don't want to listen to just what you say.
I want to feel what you mean.

I won't hold you to your words. Deep emotions
are often expressed in irrational words.

I want you to be able to say anything.

Even what you don't mean.

I am afraid of your silence because of what it could mean. Perhaps it means you are getting bored or losing interest or making up your own mind about me without my guidance. I believe that as long as I keep you talking I can know what you are thinking.

But silence can also mean confidence. And mutual respect. Silence can mean live and let live: the appreciation that I am I and you are you. This silence is an affirmation that we are already together—as two people. Words can mean that I want to make you into a friend and silence can mean that I accept your already being one.

My experience indicates that blunt honesty with my feelings gives me greater empathy with other people's feelings. My feelings appear to be a truer register of another person's feelings than my intellect. To better get at what is going on in him I sometimes ask myself not, "What is happening in him?" but "What do I *feel* is happening in him?" In order to see more clearly what he is feeling, I at times have to stop listening to what he is saying, and what I am thinking, and look inside myself. Then if I speak from this feeling within, and tell him what *I* understand him to be saying, he will usually set me straight if I have not got it right.

I must do these things in order to communicate: Become aware of you (discover you). Make you aware of me (uncover myself). Be ready to change during our conversation. And be willing to reveal my changes to you.

For communication to have meaning it must have a life. It must transcend "you and me" and become "us." If I truly communicate, I see in you a life that is not me and partake of it. And you see and partake of me. In a small way we then grow out of our old selves and become something new. To have this kind of sharing I cannot enter a conversation clutching myself. I must enter it with loose boundaries. I must give myself to the *relationship*, and be willing to be what grows out of it.

"Talking at" and "talking about" appear to be communication but are not. Gayle and I "talk about" when we go over to another couple's house and all evening the only thing said is, "Yes, and isn't it so," as if the rule were to quickly find something outside ourselves to talk about that we can all agree is terrible. The only personal comments are made while we are driving home.

Two ways I have of talking "at" other people instead of "with" them are: Talking in order to seduce them into thinking I am right, and talking in order to sound right to myself.

Last night I suddenly realized that each of us was wasting much energy trying to relate what we wanted to say to what the last person just said. A funny "should"! I see now that I was not always honest when I did this. Often I could not tell what connection had been made inside me that resulted in my wanting to say what I did, so I would manufacture a relationship to the discussion in order to be able to tell everyone a good reason for my wanting to talk. The reason was simply that I wanted to. "I want to say such-and-such. . ." not "What you said raises this question. . ."

Standard greetings and the formalities of politeness are often phony. It is a mistake, however, to conclude that following social conventions is dishonest, even if a convention is an empty form. If I am clear that my motive is to make life easier on other people, the *content* of the convention is honest.

Honesty without care is conceit.

If I want to communicate with you I must keep you informed of my feelings. A question often hides my feelings. It's sometimes my attempt to discover your position before I reveal mine, or it may hide a criticism I don't want to risk stating. If I ask you, "Why do you say that?" or "Is that what you really think?" I show you little of what I am feeling. Instead, I put you on the defensive without making clear what it is in me I want you to respond to.

The more abstract the question you ask me (Are you really happy? Do you love mankind? your country? God?), the more impossible I find it is for me to get in touch with *any feeling at all.*

I experience the feelings that make me want to open my mouth and speak, not as questions but as demands. My words spring from my emotions and my emotions are declarative, not interrogative. Even my feeling of curiosity is a statement of what I want.

"You ought to" means "I want you to," so
why not say so?

When I say "you should," I avoid committing
myself. I am referring you to some
supposedly objective standard and saying
that circumstances or decency or whatever
dictates that you do this, while I pretend to
stay out of it.

If I make you aware of all that I feel, your
reaction might give me much-needed
information about myself—or at least
about *us*.

"Let's not get personal"—Unless what you say relates to me as a person it is just words without life. But let's not just "get personal" about each other, let's get personal about ourselves.

Whether written or spoken, the more deeply personal and the more uniquely applicable people's thoughts are to their individual lives, the more I find that what they say has meaning for me. There is usually more meat for me in a writer's journals than in his or her essays.

Many people think they are acting the way they feel when they tell someone off. Someone is critical of me and I answer by calling him an S.O.B. My feeling is not that he is an S.O.B.; my feeling is that he has hurt me: "You have hurt my feelings and now I want to hurt yours." Launching a verbal attack covers my feeling of being hurt with an appearance of strength. I get angry when I think someone has changed me in a way that I am helpless to do anything about.

I get angry at Gayle when she asks me to do something if I sense that in refusing to do what she asks I will demonstrate that I am not the way I like to think of myself.

Is there a healthy anger? When I defend myself against an assault designed to destroy me, that is healthy. When I attack people because they remind me of a rejected part of myself—try to stamp out that image and throw away their feelings along with it—that is unhealthy. One response affirms and builds, the other judges and tears down.

Why can I easily get angry at Gayle and not even *feel* it toward my boss, who constantly abuses me? I must be afraid of losing something and so turn on myself to undercut the aggression. He berates me and I immediately start seeing "truth" in his criticism and so become the only weapon that can harm me.

Self-doubt forsakes power, self-betrayal forsakes the soul. I have thought that my strength would come in responding to him, but it will come in renouncing what I am doing to myself. This healthy assertion springs from self-respect and unites me. It tells me what I am and affirms my right to be it fully. My power is in my willingness to be conscious, to be seen, and to be emphatically my self. I may lose a job, a friend, or my reputation, but I lose everything I am when I fail to act from what is at the core of me.

I'm glad Gayle trusts me and our relationship enough to be able to occasionally blow up at me.

Our marriage used to suffer from arguments that were too short. Now we argue long enough to find out what the argument is about.

An argument is always about what has been made more important than the relationship.

I get along with people a lot better when I recognize that no one ever feels exactly the same about me or anyone else from one moment to the next. And, likewise, it is self-defeating to believe I must "love" anyone all of the time.

Esther may dislike me from time to time and I want to respect that by not trying to quickly change her feelings as if they were wrong.

The heart loves, but moods have no loyalty. Moods should be heard but never danced to.

If we do not exist as real people, if we are not deeply ourselves, then our relationship cannot be real.

"All I want is for you to accept me as I am."

"Yes, and all *I* want is for you to accept my not accepting you."

I want to support my friends—even in their mistakes. I must be clear, however, it is the friend and not the mistake I am supporting.

I can't assume that this woman wants to go out with me simply because I want to go out with her, but I can open my eyes and see if she does and take a reasonable risk and ask her—without trying to predetermine her answer by the way I phrase the question.

If she could choose any man she wanted she probably would not choose me, but I have been strongly attracted to women who were far from ideal and knew it. The question is not how do I compare with all men. The question is am I attractive to *this* woman at *this* time. "Am I good-looking, or too fat?"—that can't be answered, but "How is she experiencing me?" can be. To get the answer I have to look to her and not at me.

If my sexual desire for a woman is so strong and so persistent that it's getting in the way of my communication with her, I might do her, and me, a favor by telling her so. I have done this several times in my life and each time I felt the woman appreciated it (although once the husband did not). One woman surprised me by saying she felt the same, one said she did not feel that way about me, one woman did not say. Yet in all instances except the last our communication seemed freer afterwards. This approach, however, requires that I be deeply honest with myself about my motives, because so often when sex is mentioned people think they are being asked to do something. Therefore to bring this subject up can easily become, not an exercise in openness, but a deceitful manipulation. And if I truly wish to ease communication rather than make it more difficult, I must also be honest as to whether I need speak at all.

I feel attracted to Leah as she walks in the door with Bill. Now, if I am open, if I broaden my awareness to include Bill's presence, Gayle's presence, my emotions, etc., then my response will be in rhythm with the situation as a whole. It is only when I am mentally myopic that my actions become excessive or narrow.

Feelings may demand action but they do not require it. I am free to choose what my body represents. To act out does not "get it out." In fact, acting it out often reinforces the emotion and imprints it more deeply on my mind. One thing only is predictable about emotions: They will change. I don't have to "honor" every passing feeling as if an opportunity for self-fulfillment were actually slipping from my grasp.

I don't like the way I acted toward Alice. I was experiencing her as a very attractive woman, and yet the whole time I acted like a polite eunuch. When I feel my maleness sexually, I want to *consciously* decide whether to act it out. When being an asexual nice-guy is a pretense, it is also self-betrayal. A decision can come from strength or self-doubt. I see now that I want every act to be a self-affirming choice.

You say you just want to be my friend. I know that you mean you want to relate to my mind but not to my body. I can understand that and will not ask you to relate to me in a way that you don't want, or talk to me about subjects you find uncomfortable. But likewise I refuse to castrate myself for you by pretending not to have the feelings I have. If you want me as your friend you will have to accept my penis along with me.

What is the difference between "I want food" and "I want sex"?

Consent.

Let's say I want sex with a woman. If she doesn't want sex with me and I allow myself to accept this fact completely then I will probably no longer want her in that way either.

But I doubt it.

"I just can't write her off."—It's not that.
It's that I can't admit my uselessness to her,
I can't bear to be written out of *her* life.

"All I want is to be loved."—Wanting to be
loved, to be lovable, is not really a desire for
how I want to be, but for how I want others
to be.

"I need your heart and your eyes and your ears
and your touch and your words. I want you to
see me and hear me and feel me and speak to
me and love me." But by *giving* what I want,
I realize that I have what I thought I lacked
before.

Several months ago I discovered that I was interpreting a particular sensation in my abdomen as "hunger," which, when I tried listening more closely, turned out to be "tension." When I was in Berkeley I experienced very strong sensations which I interpreted as a desire for sex. Later I became close friends with several women but did not have sex with them, and these feelings lessened. I concluded that the feelings were more a desire for companionship than sex partners. Now I am in the mountains and am alone much of the time and the feelings have gone altogether (almost). It is equally logical for me to assume that in Berkeley what I really felt was a need for solitude.

The mistake I have been making is interpreting a sensation and assigning it a name ("tension," "fear," "loneliness"). This makes it autonomous, an independent force that influences me. In actuality, feelings tend to *follow* interpretation and are as varied as thoughts. Whereas a quiet mind takes form as a quiet body.

I don't *feel* "I want." I feel "I lack."
I *decide* "I want."

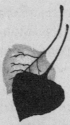

So that I will not think I am controlled by a
seemingly mindless body, I am more careful now
before making the jump from "I feel" to "I must
have." If I pause and listen closely to the
feeling, I can often hear the thought behind it,
and thoughts are easier for me to question than
feelings—because I know who is thinking them.
Cloaked in physical form, an emotion seems to
possess a certain distance and sanctity,
whereas a thought is more easily laughed at,
corrected, or replaced once it is plainly
seen.

While I am worrying about what you think of me I am not open to you, I am not letting you in; in fact, I am not letting you exist as a person—I am making you my mirror. While I am concerned with what you are thinking about me I am not even thinking about you.

I choose to use my own mind. I do not need your mind. I want to experience you, listen to you—not to myself. I have already heard everything I have to say. You are what is novel about this conversation.

In order to see I have to be willing to be seen.

If a man takes off his sunglasses I can hear him better.

As long as I'm giving you things (even "love") I don't have to notice you.

"I don't care what people think"—that is perhaps the most dishonest sentence I say to myself. Do I say it because I want to believe I don't care, or merely to give that appearance? And why is the appearance of not caring any better than vanity?

What matters is not the caring but the *way* that I care. Spending all morning in front of the bathroom mirror is not really caring what people think; it is in fact an unwillingness to let people think. The attention I give to what I wear, the length of my hair, how much I weigh, etc., is designed to *control* what people will think.

If I would spend half the time preparing my mind that I do preparing my body, perhaps I would have the ease that my effecting appearance is supposed to produce for me.

I used to dislike social functions to the point that I considered myself a sincere misanthrope. What I didn't realize was that I hated having to shield myself, the hard and unpleasant work of acting without acknowledging it. Now that I feel freer to let myself alone and allow others to like or dislike me as they choose, I have lost much of this aversion.

A stimulus can be used any way I decide. The sight of another person can be my cue to relax. The sight of a crowd can be my cue to peace.

I learn most about myself by observing myself in relation to others. When I examine myself by myself I am actually examining the results of a previous encounter.

Perceptions are not of things but of relationships. Nothing, including me, exists by itself—this is an illusion of words. I *am* a relationship, ever-expanding.

I walk down the street and the guy waiting for the bus—who has been waiting there for God knows how long—suddenly finds something more interesting to look at than a live human being. I do the same.

Do I avoid looking a stranger in the eyes because I don't want to make him uncomfortable, or do I turn my eyes so he can't look into me?

Is there a way of seeing that does not need eyes? Is there a way of touching that does not need hands? Is there a way of loving that is beyond words and time spent, beyond prescribed greetings and reciprocity? If there is, I am ready for it now.

Something within me will not let me rest with a bad opinion of another person. Dislike is for me an unpleasant sensation. It distresses me to hear someone criticize another person, and I feel uneasy when I join in. Hatred seems to be its own punishment, but something in me rejoices in a newfound appreciation. As an act of faith, as a response to something that feels very deep in me, I believe this about other human beings: Regardless of their present mood (which I wish to respect) they want to be my friend. For no other reason than I am also human, they want to feel love for me and want me to feel love for them. Deep within them they want to be close to me and to all living things. This faith does not require that I do anything overt, it requires only that I not forget.

One thing has become quite clear: All acquaintances are passing. Therefore I want to make the most of every contact. I want to quickly get close to the people I meet because my experience has shown we won't be together long.

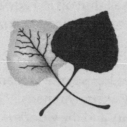

People in cars passing by my car, people walking past me on the street, someone leaving a shop as I enter, Gayle coming through the door from work, Willie getting his mail as I get mine, and with each one of these little brushings-against, these encounters big and small, I leave something behind. If I can feel what I pick up from them, certainly on some level they can feel my state also. What, then, is the trail behind me composed of? Does not this "gift to the world," by its very enormity, outweigh all others?

How much do I really love *people*? If I had
been cut off from people for twenty or thirty years—
totally cut off—I would love to hear the
yelling upstairs, the screaming of the
children, the barking dog, the loud music. I
would not want it all shut off as I went to
sleep, but would savor it even as I dozed off.

"I am one with nature" so often means
wanting to get away from humans. If loving
to be in the country and the woods is being
"one with nature" then loving to be in the
city and the malls is being "one with people."

I love people when I love them for being
people, and not for being young or old or
beautiful or hip. I wish I could love what
humanity has built just because humanity has
built it: streets, power lines, buildings,
cars. It's easy to love nature. Why? I have
been taught that God made trees. But is that
all God made? Art, grace, melody, beauty, are
a way of looking. Why isn't traffic music to
me, and music noise?

Love unites the part with the whole. Love unites me with the world and with myself. My life work could well be love. Love is the universe complete. Detachment is the universe divided. Detachment divides me from myself and from others. Love is the vision that can see all as one and one as all: "I and my father are one." Is there but one reality and one truth? Love shows me where all minds and essences unite.

How do I get love? I have it. I must drop my definitions of love. Love is not saying nice things to people or smiling or doing good deeds. Love is love. Don't strive for love, be it.

All my life I have made it complicated, but it is so simple. I love when I love. And when I love, I am my self.

There is a certain beauty in poverty, loss, and desolation. There is a certain strength and grandeur in suffering. Grays, storms, ruins, age, are powerful subjects for a painting. Even a dump heap can evoke admiration.

When I look at the world gently, when I look at others the way I have sometimes sensed that Something looks at me, I become a friend. And there is no higher calling.

It is not that there are no accidents, evil, deformity, pettiness, hatred. It's that there *is* a broader view. Evil exists in the part. Perfection exists in the whole. Sin is seeing nearsightedly. And I can choose this broader view—not that I always will—but I always can.

Ideas are clean. They soar in the serene
supernal. I can take them out and look
at them, they fit in books, they lead me
down that narrow way. And in the morning they are there. Ideas are straight—

But the world is round, and a
messy mortal is my friend.

Come walk with me in the mud. . . . .

To the reader:

I enjoyed writing this book, but now I am feeling some limitations in it, and I want you to know my reservations.

First, my notes sometimes sound like axioms, and I question the helpfulness of self-evident truths, even my own. Truth is not a *statement*, and yet I can remember times during the writing when I believed I was presenting truth. There are statements I have heard or read that have come back to me from time to time, and some that had little meaning when I ingested them later surfaced with surprising force, but no set of words has retained constant value for me, and none was but a shadow of the reality it pointed to.

Second, I keep thinking of exceptions to what I have written, or maybe they are additions, maybe both are true. For example, last night I heard myself say to a man, "Let's not get personal," in apparent contradiction to what I had written in one of my notes. What I had come to realize was that my style of being congruent just wasn't working with this person. Yet he took this mild reprimand, and even called himself on it several times afterwards. A strictly abstract discussion followed and lasted for several hours. It greatly pleased him, and it brought us closer together than we had ever been.

My third point concerns the times in this book I speak of my "choosing" the positive in me to act on instead of the negative, but frankly I don't experience "choice," "decision," and "will" as the neat packages their names imply. "I decide" suggests a starting point, a spontaneous creation, whereas what I experience within me is more a flow, a flow that has always been going on. I flow in one direction and not in another, and as I notice this direction I say to myself, "I have decided." If choice were in reality the selecting of one part of me over another then my decisions would divide me and alienate the unchosen parts. What I see in my life is an ever-deepening awareness that unites me as it goes to the core of me. My awareness deepens *and* my behavior becomes more positive. I experience depth of awareness and degree of positiveness as one thing. "Choice" implies that they are separate and so makes the "will" appear more important than it is.

The fourth point is that I keep seeing a "higher truth," and this disturbs my sense of having completed this book. For example, I talk about accepting my feelings and not condemning myself for the negative ones, but I am wondering now if all feelings are not equally useful when acknowledged. Grief, worry, doubt, and suffering at times can act almost like faithful intuitions that set me straight. In this book I talk about how boredom has sometimes enlarged my range of options. I recently found that tiredness can be a delicious feeling if I value it. And a few weeks ago I discovered that by appreciating a feeling of revenge I got in touch with my compassion. It happened like this: After receiving a great deal of strident criticism from a man, I found that I was having many spontaneous revenge fantasies.

I tried to accept these but felt I was stuck and that nothing productive was happening. Then it occurred to me to do something more than just accept my fantasies. I tried going with them. I tried to enjoy them and to make them even bigger and more outrageous. And a surprising thing happened. After I had created a particularly violent ending to a fantasy, I suddenly saw this person in an entirely new light—I saw his side—and I felt an understanding and warmth for him that I had not experienced before.

I am no longer so sure that what is so often called "love" is *the* greatest thing in the world, that it is any better for me or for those to whom I express it than, say, anger. Other people's anger, especially when I can get past reacting defensively, has taught me some unforgettable lessons. I don't think I would choose to have those moments replaced by "love." Faith in what is happening inside another seems more valid an attitude than discrimination. If there is any good, I have to see it first in me, and then live what I see. I do not need more to believe. I already believe enough. What I need is the willingness to try out the contents of my own heart.

Now if it is true—and I am not yet sure that it is—that I will come to appreciate all my feelings as they are, and not just accept them, but see them as innocent indicators, then I need to rewrite much of this book. But if I do that, of course I will no longer be at the same level of learning that I am now, and as my vision changes, the thoughts that are helpful will change with it. The answer must be for me to use an idea as long as it is usable and not be afraid to let go of it when it has served its purpose. Thoughts and books, sometimes great religions and certain people, provide me with a broader view, but then I feel a familiar homesickness and I know that the time has come for me to move on, taking them with me, but no longer stopping at the boundary of their words.

The fifth point I want to make is that the writing in this book is an expression of insights on my current *problems*. As I write I am in a state of learning, becoming, arriving, and not in a state of knowing and having arrived. I write about communication because I find it hard to talk to people. I write about my sexual desires because I am learning to cope with them. Therefore what I have here is of necessity imperfect and halting, a grasping for knowledge but not knowledge. I notice that I sometimes use superlatives to impress a new discovery on me like a child beating his head "to get it through his thick skull." I sometimes use generalizations in the same way, or sometimes to broaden the hegemony of my "truth," or sometimes to convince you—to cause you to accept my truth for yours, and thereby gain the illusion of expanding my self. Often writing serves the same purpose for me as arguing—a testing to see if the ideas can bear scrutiny, but at times it goes even further and is a cry for us to be done with ideas and know peace.

The last point I want to make is crucial to the understanding of this book. I have seen honesty or "being real" act sometimes like a new religion, a new form of self-justification, a new perfectionism, or even a perverse new snobbery. I experienced this recently when I found myself arguing against someone else's sense of truth on the grounds that his truth was imposed by an outside authority whereas *I knew* that all truth must come from within. I was in effect shouting down his throat: "You shouldn't be telling me what I shouldn't be," or "I won't accept your not believing in acceptance." I also sense that I am misusing the idea of honesty whenever I discover myself anxiously weighing my words and actions, that is, whenever I am being very careful to be "real." When I do this I am only playing a new role—the role of the "real person." Calculation does not enter into being real. Concern with appearances does not enter into it. Being real is more a process of letting go than it is the effort of becoming. I don't really have to become my self, although at times it feels this way. I already am what I am. And that is both the simplest and the hardest thing for me to realize.

Hugh Prather
July 1970
Chama, New Mexico

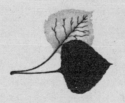

ABOUT THE AUTHOR

In 1968 Hugh Prather asked his wife, Gayle, if she would support both of them from her teacher's salary while he devoted his full time to writing. She agreed, but two years later nothing that he had submitted had been accepted. He decided to try a book composed of excerpts from his diary, set in the same short-paragraph format in which he wrote to himself. The manuscript was sent to a newly formed husband-and-wife publishing venture in California that had published only three other books, ran no ads, and had no sales representatives. It took *Notes to Myself* three years to work its way across country and become a national best-seller. It has since been published in numerous foreign editions and audio cassette, and twenty years later continues to sell at best-seller rates.

After the publication of his first book, Hugh increasingly turned to Gayle as a co-author in an attempt to present a more balanced and gentle message in the many books that followed. The diaries were continued with *I Touch the Earth, the Earth Touches Me* and *Notes on Love and Courage,* followed by a trilogy of reflections on *A Course in Miracles: There Is a Place Where You Are Not Alone, A Book of Games,* and *The Quiet Answer.* During this period the Prathers were becoming increasingly involved in counseling within the field of domestic crisis: alcoholics, battered women, and especially parents of children who had died. In an attempt to help in a deeper way, they founded The Dispensable Church and wrote, *Notes on How to Live in the World . . . and Still Be Happy, A Book for Couples,* and, coming full circle, *Notes to Each Other,* three books that come from years of workshop and counseling experience and from the work they have done within their own twenty-five-year marriage.

Hugh and Gayle and their two boys, John and Jordan, live in the hills of Aptos, California, together with eight chickens, three goldfish, two rabbits, their cat, Tuba, and their dog, Kokomo Jones.

"To me, Hugh Prather speaks the language of spiritual transformation. I love this man—and all that he writes."

—*Wayne W. Dyer, author of* You'll See It When You Believe It

"Inspiring, insightful, and integrating. Maturing adulthood at its very best!"

—*W. Brugh Joy, M.D., SACP, author of* Joy's Way: A Map for the Transformation Journey

"I first read *Notes to Myself* about twenty years ago. It gave me a boost in my journey of personal growth. It is a precious jewel."

—*Ken Keyes, Jr., author of* Handbook to Higher Consciousness *and* The Hundredth Monkey

"*Notes to Myself* is an excellent introduction to basic self-awareness. Written from the heart with genuine authenticity, it invites acceptance and love. Prather's refreshing perspective on the struggles of everyday life is a gift of practical wisdom for all of us."

—*Frances Vaughan, author of* The Inward Arc: Healing and Wholeness in Psychotherapy and Spirituality

"Twenty years ago, *Notes to Myself* helped usher in the New Age; today it is a classic, as relevant and contemporary as ever. Its searching honesty can open the way to personal enlightenment for anyone."

—*Arnold R. Beisser, author of* Flying Without Wings

"Lao-tzu tells us: To know others is intelligent; to know ourselves is true wisdom. Hugh Prather's insightful personal search and cultivation in this classic little gem is a wonder of human nature."

—Chungliang Al Huang,
founder, Living Tao Foundation, and author of Embrace Tiger, Return to Mountain, and Tai Ji

"Most of the world's books are never read at all by the great majority of the human race. Others are read but once. A third and quite rare category consists of books that may be referred to repeatedly. Such a book is Notes to Myself. It can and should be often enjoyed."

—Steve Allen, comedian, composer, and author

"Reading Notes to Myself the first time was like putting on a new pair of glasses that helped drastically to improve my vision. Now reading the revised edition has reminded me of how dirty my glasses have become. Thanks, Hugh, for coming along to clean my glasses."

—Wally "Famous" Amos, cookie magnate and author of The Power in You

"To Hugh Prather, the soft thudding sound you hear is our footsteps following you joyfully and gratefully."

—Elizabeth and Robert Young

"Reading this volume . . . has been most rewarding. . . . After only a few pages I was put into a powerfully reflective mood that brought me to the mode of "true reality." It was difficult to put the book down. . . . The short reflections are just what we need to center our thoughts for meditation. . . . I am sure that it will bring the experience of peace to anyone who takes the time to examine it. . . . *Notes to Myself* . . . has become part of my daily spiritual diet."

—*Friar Justin Belitz, O.F.M.*

"*Notes to Myself* is a timeless gem. Hugh Prather's insights and honest evaluation of his innermost thoughts reflected many of my own. This book serves as an indispensable guide to the actualization of the higher self."

—*Paul Horn, musician and composer*

"What a wonderful breath of fresh air!"

—*Robert A. Johnson,*
author of He, She, *and* We

"This lustrous classic touched my life many years ago, and its powerful insights are even more meaningful today. It's a national treasure."

—*Og Mandino,*
author of The Greatest Salesman in the World

"*Notes to Myself* helped initiate me into the human potential movement and deeper self-acceptance. This is a classic, landmark book."

—*Harold H. Bloomfield, M.D.,*
author of How to Survive the Loss of a Love

"*Notes to Myself* will be remembered not as one man's inquiry into himself, but as a monumental journey of discovery the whole human race has embarked upon."

—*Barry Vissell, M.D., and Joyce Vissell, R.N., M.S., coauthors of* The Shared Heart

"Hugh Prather's *Notes to Myself* is a powerful collection of affirmative statements and meaningful insights that can inspire anyone who is reaching for more light while standing in the darkness. I've often given his book instead of advice."

—*Jack Boland, Unity minister*

"Hugh Prather describes the meaning of life in a simple and engaging way. He is truly the consummate writer. His books are alive, meaningful and helpful guides because he tells the truth and is committed to serve us with his zest and love for life. His readers love him because they feel his love for them."

—*Arnold M. Patent, author of* You Can Have It All

"When I first read *Notes to Myself* several years ago, a deep bell of remembering rang within me and I had this freeing feeling: 'Why didn't I write these notes to myself? But since I didn't, couldn't, wouldn't—God bless you, Hugh Prather, for doing it for me!' May this 20th Anniversary edition ring bells of freedom and joy in the soul of every reader!"

—*J. Sig Paulson, Unity minister*

"I am a painter. A painter's ego is particularly vulnerable. Each time he shows a new work he offers himself up to sometimes brutal criticism—even from himself. This little book has helped me in . . . my struggle to keep things in perspective and preserve my self-esteem."

—*Clark Hulings*